QUICK & EASY RECIPES FOR

BREAKFAST

Tina Collins

Table of Contents

BREAKFAST 7

Prosciutto, Mozzarella & Eggs in a Cup 8

Crustless Mediterranean Quiche 10

Air Fried Italian Calzone 12

Italian Sausage Patties 14

Brioche Toast with Chocolate 16

Omelet Bread Cups 18

Kiwi Muffins with Pecans 20

Hearty Banana Pastry 22

Mango Bread 23

Pumpkin & Sultanas' Bread 25

French Toast with Vanilla Filling 27

Greek-Style Frittata 29

Egg Bites 31

Spinach Sausage Egg Muffins 33

Cheese Pepper Egg Bake.................................35

Almond Broccoli Muffins 37

Italian Breakfast Frittata 39

Fresh Herb Egg Cups....................................41

Feta Pepper Egg Muffins 43

Vanilla Raspberry Muffins 45

Breakfast Bake Egg 47

Easy Chicken Egg Cups................................ 49

Easy Breakfast Sausage 51

Zucchini Breakfast Casserole 53

Basil Cheese Zucchini Quiche 55

Asparagus Quiche..57

Moist Pumpkin Muffins.................................59

Healthy Zucchini Gratin............................... 61

Artichoke Quiche 63

Tomato Feta Frittata....................................65

Blueberry Cream Cheese Toasts....................67

Onion & Cheddar Omelet 69

Spicy Egg & Bacon Tortilla Wraps 71

Turkey & Mushroom Sandwich................................73

Grilled Tofu Sandwich with Cabbage...........................75

Buttered Eggs in Hole...77

Loaded Egg Pepper Rings.......................................78

Chili Hash Browns 80

Japanese-Style Omelet 82

Baked Kale Omelet.. 84

Baked Avocado with Eggs & Cilantro..........................85

Cheese Egg Quiche...87

Chorizo Casserole 89

Sausage Egg Omelet...91

Cheese Ham Egg Muffins 93

Perfect Baked Omelet 95

Broccoli Casserole...97

THANK YOU.. 99

BREAKFAST

Prosciutto, Mozzarella & Eggs in a Cup

Prep + cook time: 20 minutes 2 servings

Ingredients

- 2 bread slices

- 2 prosciutto slices, chopped

- 2 eggs

- 4 tomato slices

- ¼ tsp balsamic vinegar

- 2 tbsp mozzarella cheese, grated

- ¼ tsp maple syrup

- 2 tbsp mayonnaise

- Salt and black pepper to taste

- Cooking spray

Directions

Preheat air fryer to 350 F. Grease 2 ramekins with cooking spray. Place one bread slice on the bottom of each ramekin. Place 2 tomato slices on top and divide mozzarella cheese between the ramekins. Crack the eggs over the mozzarella cheese. Drizzle with maple syrup and balsamic vinegar. Season with salt and pepper and Bake for 10 minutes in the fryer. Top with mayonnaise and serve.

Crustless Mediterranean Quiche

Prep + cook time: 40 minutes 2 servings

Ingredients

- 4 eggs

- ½ cup tomatoes, chopped

- 1 cup feta cheese, crumbled

- ½ tbsp fresh basil, chopped

- ½ tbsp fresh oregano, chopped

- ¼ cup Kalamata olives, sliced

- ¼ cup onions, chopped

- ½ cup milk

- Salt and black pepper to taste

Directions

Preheat air fryer to 340 F. Beat the eggs along with the milk, salt, and pepper. Stir in all the remaining ingredients. Pour the egg mixture into a greased baking pan that fits in your air fryer and place in the fryer. Bake for 30 minutes or until lightly golden. Serve warm with a green salad.

Air Fried Italian Calzone

Prep + cook time: 20 minutes 4 servings

Ingredients

- 1 pizza dough
- 4 oz cheddar cheese, grated
- 1 oz mozzarella cheese, grated
- 1 oz bacon, diced
- 2 cups cooked turkey, shredded
- 1 egg, beaten
- 4 tbsp tomato paste
- ½ tsp dried basil
- ½ tsp dried oregano
- Salt and black pepper to taste

Directions

Preheat air fryer to 350 F. Divide the pizza dough into 4 equal pieces, so you have the dough for 4 pizza crusts. Combine the tomato paste, basil, and oregano in a small bowl. Brush the mixture onto the crusts; make sure not to go all the way and avoid brushing near the edges of each crust. Scatter half of the turkey on top and season with salt and pepper. Top with bacon, mozzarella and cheddar cheeses. Brush the edges with the beaten egg. Fold the crusts and seal with a fork. Bake for 10-12 minutes until puffed and golden, turning over halfway through the cooking time. Serve.

Italian Sausage Patties

Prep + cook time: 20 minutes 4 servings

Ingredients

- 1 lb ground Italian sausage

- ¼ cup breadcrumbs

- 1 tsp red pepper flakes

- Salt and black pepper to taste

- ¼ tsp garlic powder

- 1 egg, beaten

Directions

Preheat air fryer to 350 F. Combine all the ingredients in a large bowl. Make patties out of the mixture and arrange them on a greased baking sheet. Add to the fryer and AirFry for 15 minutes, flipping once.

Brioche Toast with Chocolate

Prep + cook time: 15 minutes 2 servings

Ingredients

- 4 slices of brioche

- 3 eggs

- 4 tbsp butter

- 6 oz milk chocolate, broken into chunks

- ½ cup heavy cream

- 1 tsp vanilla extract

- ½ cup maple syrup

- ½ tsp salt

Directions

Preheat air fryer to 350 F. Beat the eggs with heavy cream, salt, and vanilla in a small bowl. Dip the brioche slices in the egg mixture and AirFry in the greased fryer for 7-8 minutes in total, shaking once or twice. Melt the chocolate and butter in the microwave for 60-90 seconds, remove, and whisk with a fork until well combined. Let cool slightly. When the brioches are ready, remove, and dip in the chocolate-butter mixture. Serve with a cup of tea and enjoy!

Omelet Bread Cups

Prep + cook time: 25 minutes 4 servings

Ingredients

- 4 crusty rolls
- 5 eggs, beaten
- ½ tsp thyme, dried
- 3 strips cooked bacon, chopped
- 2 tbsp heavy cream
- 4 Gouda cheese thin slices

Directions

Preheat air fryer to 330 F. Cut the tops off the rolls and remove the inside with your fingers. Line the rolls with a slice of cheese and press down, so the cheese conforms to the inside of the roll.

In a bowl, mix the eggs, heavy cream, bacon, and thyme. Stuff the rolls with the egg mixture. Lay them in the greased air fryer's basket and bake for 8-10 minutes or until the eggs become puffy, and the roll shows a golden brown texture. Remove and serve immediately.

Kiwi Muffins with Pecans

Prep + cook time: 25 minutes 4 servings

Ingredients

- 1 cup flour

- 1 kiwi, mashed

- ¼ cup powdered sugar

- 1 tsp milk

- 1 tbsp pecans, chopped

- ½ tsp baking powder

- ¼ cup oats

- ¼ cup butter, room temperature

Directions

Preheat air fryer to 350 F. Place the sugar, pecans, kiwi, and butter in a bowl and mix well. In another bowl, mix the flour, baking powder, and oats and stir well. Combine the two mixtures and stir in the milk. Pour the batter into a greased muffin tin that fits in the fryer and Bake for 15 minutes. Remove to a wire rack and leave to cool for a few minutes before removing from the muffin tin. Enjoy!

Hearty Banana Pastry

Prep + cook time: 20 minutes 2 servings

Ingredients

- 3 bananas, sliced
- 3 tbsp honey
- 2 puff pastry sheets, cut into thin strips
- 1 cup fresh berries to serve

Directions

Preheat air fryer to 340 F. Place the banana slices into a greased baking dish. Cover with pastry strips and drizzle with honey. Bake in the air fryer for 12 minutes until golden. Serve with berries.

Mango Bread

Prep + cook time: 30 minutes 6 servings

Ingredients

- ½ cup butter, melted
- 1 egg, lightly beaten
- ½ cup brown sugar
- 1 tsp vanilla extract
- 3 ripe mangoes, mashed
- 1 ½ cups flour
- 1 tsp baking powder
- ½ tsp grated nutmeg
- ½ tsp ground cinnamon

Directions

Line a loaf tin with baking paper. In a bowl, whisk melted butter, egg, sugar, vanilla, and mangoes. Sift in flour, baking powder, nutmeg, and ground cinnamon and stir without overmixing. Pour the batter into the tin and place it in the air fryer. Bake for 18-20 minutes at 330 F. Let cool before slicing and serve.

Pumpkin & Sultanas' Bread

Prep + cook time: 30 minutes + cooling time 6 servings

Ingredients

- 1 cup pumpkin, peeled and shredded
- 1 cup flour
- 1 tsp ground nutmeg
- ½ tsp salt
- ¼ tsp baking powder
- 2 eggs
- ½ cup sugar
- ¼ cup milk
- 2 tbsp butter, melted
- ½ tsp vanilla extract
- 2 tbsp sultanas, soaked

- 1 tbsp honey

- 1 tbsp canola oil

Directions

Preheat air fryer to 350 F. In a bowl, beat the eggs and add in pumpkin, sugar, milk, canola oil, sultanas, and vanilla. In a separate bowl, sift the flour and mix in nutmeg, salt, butter, and baking powder. Combine the 2 mixtures and stir until a thick cake mixture forms. Spoon the batter into a greased baking dish and place it in the air fryer. Bake for 25 minutes until a toothpick inserted in the center comes out clean and dry. Remove to a wire rack to cool completely. Drizzle with honey and serve.

French Toast with Vanilla Filling

Prep + cook time: 15 minutes 3 servings

Ingredients

- 6 slices white bread

- 2 eggs

- ¼ cup heavy cream

- 1/3 cup sugar mixed with

- 1 tsp ground cinnamon

- 6 tbsp caramel

- 1 tsp vanilla extract

- Cooking spray

DIRECTIONS In a bowl, whisk eggs, and heavy cream. Dip each piece of bread into the egg mixture. Coat the bread with sugar and cinnamon mixture. On a clean board, lay the coated slices and spread three of the slices with about 2 tbsp of caramel each around the center. Place the remaining three slices on top to form three sandwiches. Spray the air fryer basket with some cooking spray. Arrange the sandwiches into the fryer and cook for 10 minutes at 340 F, turning once

Greek-Style Frittata

Prep + cook time: 30 minutes 4 servings

Ingredients

- 5 eggs
- 1 cup baby spinach
- ½ cup grape tomatoes, halved
- ½ cup feta cheese, crumbled
- 10 Kalamata olives, sliced
- Salt and black pepper to taste
- 2 tbsp fresh parsley, chopped

DIRECTIONS Preheat air fryer to 360 F. Beat the eggs, salt, and pepper in a bowl, combining well before adding the spinach and stirring until all is mixed. Pour half the mixture into a greased baking pan. On top of the mixture, add half of the tomatoes, olives, and feta. Cover the pan with foil, making sure to close it tightly around the edges, then place the pan in the air fryer and cook for 12 minutes. Remove the foil and cook for an additional 5-7 minutes, until the eggs are fully cooked. Place the finished frittata on a serving plate and repeat the above instructions for the remainder of the ingredients. Decorate with parsley and cut into wedges. Serve hot or at room temperature.

Egg Bites

Preparation Time: 10 minutes Cooking Time: 10 minutes Serve: 4

Ingredients:

- 4 eggs

- 1/4 cup cheddar cheese, shredded

- 4 bacon slices, cooked and crumbled

- 1/2 bell pepper, diced

- 1/2 onion, diced

- 1 tbsp unsweetened almond milk

- Pepper Salt

Directions:

In a bowl, whisk eggs with cheese, milk, pepper, and salt. Stir in bacon, bell pepper, and onion. Pour egg mixture into the 4 silicone muffin molds. Select Air Fry mode. Set time to 10 minutes and temperature 300 F then press START. The air fryer display will prompt you to ADD FOOD once the temperature is reached then place muffin molds in the air fryer basket. Serve and enjoy.

Spinach Sausage Egg Muffins

Preparation Time: 10 minutes Cooking Time: 20 minutes Serve: 6

Ingredients:

- 2 eggs

- 5 egg whites

- 3 lean breakfast turkey sausage

- 1/4 cup cheddar cheese, shredded

- 1/4 cup spinach, chopped

- 1/4 cup unsweetened almond milk

- Pepper Salt

Directions:

In a pan, brown the turkey sausage over medium-high heat until sausage is brown. Cut sausage in small pieces and set aside. In a bowl, whisk eggs, egg whites, milk, pepper, and salt. Stir in spinach. Pour egg mixture into the silicone muffin molds. Divide sausage and cheese evenly between each muffin mold. Select Bake mode. Set time to 20 minutes and temperature 350 F then press START. The air fryer display will prompt you to ADD FOOD once the temperature is reached then place muffin molds in the air fryer basket. Serve and enjoy

Cheese Pepper Egg Bake

Preparation Time: 10 minutes Cooking Time: 30 minutes Serve: 2

Ingredients:

- 3 eggs

- 1/2 cup cottage cheese

- 1 1/2 tbsp jalapeno, chopped

- 1/2 cup pepper jack cheese, shredded

- 1/8 tsp pepper

- 1/8 tsp sea salt

Directions:

In a bowl, whisk eggs with pepper and salt. Stir in jalapeno, pepper jack cheese, and cottage cheese. Pour egg mixture into the greased 7-inch baking dish. Cover dish with foil. Select Bake mode. Set time to 30 minutes and temperature 350 F then press START. The air fryer display will prompt you to ADD FOOD once the temperature is reached then place the baking dish in the air fryer basket. Serve and enjoy.

Almond Broccoli Muffins

Preparation Time: 10 minutes Cooking Time: 30 minutes Serve: 6

Ingredients:

- 2 eggs

- 1 cup broccoli florets, chopped

- 1 cup unsweetened almond milk

- 1 cup coconut flour

- 1 cup almond flour

- 1 tsp baking powder

- 2 tbsp nutritional yeast

- 1/2 tsp sea salt

Directions:

Add all ingredients into the large bowl and mix until well combined. Pour batter into the silicone muffin molds. Select Bake mode. Set time to 30 minutes and temperature 350 F then press START. The air fryer display will prompt you to ADD FOOD once the temperature is reached then place muffin molds in the air fryer basket. Serve and enjoy.

Italian Breakfast Frittata

Preparation Time: 10 minutes Cooking Time: 30 minutes Serve: 6

Ingredients:

- 6 eggs

- 3/4 cup mozzarella cheese, shredded

- 1/4 cup fresh basil, chopped

- 1/2 cup tomatoes, chopped

- 1 tsp Italian seasoning

- 2 tbsp water

- Pepper Salt

Directions:

In a bowl, whisk eggs with water, 1/2 cheese, Italian seasoning, pepper, and salt. Stir in remaining cheese, basil, and tomatoes. Pour egg mixture into the greased 8-inch pie dish. Cover dish with foil. Select Bake mode. Set time to 30 minutes and temperature 350 F then press

START. The air fryer display will prompt you to ADD FOOD once the temperature is reached then place the pie dish in the air fryer basket. Serve and enjoy.

Fresh Herb Egg Cups

Preparation Time: 10 minutes Cooking Time: 20 minutes Serve: 6

Ingredients:

- 6 eggs

- 1 tbsp fresh parsley, chopped

- 1 tbsp chives, chopped

- 1 tbsp fresh basil, chopped

- 1 tbsp fresh cilantro, chopped

- 1/4 cup mozzarella cheese, grated

- 1 tbsp fresh dill, chopped

- Pepper Salt

Directions:

In a bowl, whisk eggs with pepper and salt. Add remaining ingredients and stir well. Pour egg mixture into the silicone muffin molds. Select Bake mode. Set time to 20 minutes and temperature 350 F then press START. The air fryer display will prompt you to ADD FOOD once the temperature is reached then place muffin molds in the air fryer basket. Serve and enjoy.

Feta Pepper Egg Muffins

Preparation Time: 10 minutes Cooking Time: 20 minutes Serve: 12

Ingredients:

- 4 eggs

- 1/2 cup egg whites

- 1 tsp garlic powder

- 2 tbsp feta cheese, crumbled

- 2 tbsp green onion, chopped

- 4 fresh basil leaves, chopped

- 1/4 cup unsweetened coconut milk

- 1 red bell pepper, chopped

- Pepper Salt

Directions:

In a bowl, whisk eggs, egg whites, milk, garlic powder, pepper, and salt. Stir in cheese, bell pepper, green onion, and basil. Pour egg mixture into the silicone muffin molds. Select Bake mode. Set time to 20 minutes and temperature 350 F then press START. The air fryer display will prompt you to ADD FOOD once the temperature is reached then place muffin molds in the air fryer basket. Serve and enjoy.

Vanilla Raspberry Muffins

Preparation Time: 10 minutes Cooking Time: 20 minutes Serve: 12

Ingredients:

3 eggs

1/2 cup raspberries

1/2 tsp vanilla

1/3 cup unsweetened almond milk

1/3 cup coconut oil, melted

1 1/2 tsp baking powder

1/2 cup Swerve

2 1/2 cups almond flour

Directions:

In a large bowl, mix almond flour, baking powder, and sweetener. Stir in the coconut oil, vanilla, eggs, and almond milk. Add raspberries and fold well. Pour mixture into the silicone muffin molds. Select Bake mode. Set time to 20 minutes and temperature 350 F then press START. The air fryer display will prompt you to ADD FOOD once the temperature is reached then place muffin molds in the air fryer basket. Serve and enjoy.

Breakfast Bake Egg

Preparation Time: 10 minutes Cooking Time: 15 minutes Serve: 1

Ingredients:

- 2 eggs

- 2 tbsp cheddar cheese, shredded

- 2 tbsp half and half

- 1 tbsp parmesan cheese, grated

- 1/2 tsp garlic powder

- Pepper Salt

Directions:

In a small bowl, whisk eggs and a half and half. Stir in cheddar cheese, parmesan cheese, pepper, and salt. Pour egg mixture into the greased 8-ounce ramekin. Select Bake mode. Set time to 15 minutes and temperature 400 F then press START. The air fryer display will prompt you to ADD FOOD once the temperature is reached then place the ramekin in the air fryer basket. Serve and enjoy.

Easy Chicken Egg Cups

Preparation Time: 10 minutes Cooking Time: 15 minutes Serve: 12

Ingredients:

- 10 eggs

- 1 cup chicken, cooked and chopped

- 1/2 tsp garlic powder

- 1/4 tsp pepper

- 1 tsp sea salt

Directions:

In a large bowl, whisk eggs with pepper and salt. Add remaining ingredients and stir well. Pour egg mixture into the silicone muffin molds. Select Bake mode. Set time to 15 minutes and temperature 400 F then press START. The air fryer display will prompt you to ADD FOOD once the temperature is reached then place muffin molds in the air fryer basket. Serve and enjoy.

Easy Breakfast Sausage

Preparation Time: 10 minutes Cooking Time: 15 minutes Serve: 6

Ingredients:

- 2 lbs ground pork
- 1 tbsp dried parsley
- 1 tbsp Italian seasoning
- 2 tbsp olive oil
- 1 tsp paprika
- 1 tsp red pepper flakes
- 2 tsp salt

Directions:

In a large bowl, combine together ground pork, paprika, red pepper flakes, parsley, Italian seasoning, olive oil, pepper, and salt. Make small patties from the meat mixture. Place the cooking tray in the air fryer basket. Line air fryer basket with parchment paper. Select Bake mode. Set time to 15 minutes and temperature 375 F then press START. The air fryer display will prompt you to ADD FOOD once the temperature is reached then place patties onto the parchment paper in the air fryer basket. Serve and enjoy.

Zucchini Breakfast Casserole

Preparation Time: 10 minutes Cooking Time: 50 minutes Serve: 8

Ingredients:

- 12 eggs
- 2 small zucchinis, shredded
- 1 lb ground Italian sausage
- 3 tomatoes, sliced
- 3 tbsp coconut flour
- 1/4 cup unsweetened almond milk
- 1/4 tsp pepper
- 1/2 tsp salt

Directions:

Cook sausage in a pan until lightly brown. Transfer sausage to a large bowl. Add coconut flour, milk, eggs, zucchini, pepper, and salt and mix well. Add eggs and whisk until well combined. Pour egg mixture into the greased casserole dish and top with tomato slices. Cover dish with foil. Select Bake mode. Set time to 50 minutes and temperature 350 F then press START. The air fryer display will prompt you to ADD FOOD once the temperature is reached then place a casserole dish in the air fryer basket. Serve and enjoy.

Basil Cheese Zucchini Quiche

Preparation Time: 10 minutes Cooking Time: 40 minutes Serve: 6

Ingredients:

- 3 eggs

- 1 cup mozzarella, shredded

- 15 oz ricotta

- 1 onion, chopped

- 2 medium zucchinis, sliced

- 1/2 tsp dried oregano

- 1/2 tsp dried basil

- 1 tbsp olive oil

- Black pepper Salt

Directions:

Heat oil in a pan over medium heat. Add zucchini and sauté over low heat. Add onion and cook for 10 minutes. Add pepper and seasoning. In a bowl, whisk eggs. Stir in mozzarella, ricotta, onions, and zucchini. Pour egg mixture into the greased pie dish. Cover dish with foil. Select Bake mode. Set time to 30 minutes and temperature 350 F then press START. The air fryer display will prompt you to ADD FOOD once the temperature is reached then place the pie dish in the air fryer basket. Serve and enjoy.

Asparagus Quiche

Preparation Time: 10 minutes Cooking Time: 30 minutes Serve: 6

Ingredients:

- 4 eggs
- 4 egg whites
- 1/4 cup water
- 8 oz asparagus, cut into 1-inch pieces
- 2 tbsp feta cheese, crumbled
- 1 cup cottage cheese
- 1/2 tsp dried thyme
- 1/4 tsp pepper
- 1/4 tsp salt

Directions:

Add water into the large pot and bring to boil over high heat. Add asparagus into the pot and cook for 2 minutes.

Drain well. In a large bowl, whisk egg whites, eggs, cottage cheese, thyme, water, pepper, and salt. Pour egg mixture into the greased baking dish. Add asparagus pieces into the egg mixture and top with feta cheese. Cover dish with foil. Select Bake mode. Set time to 30 minutes and temperature 375 F then press START. The air fryer display will prompt you to ADD FOOD once the temperature is reached then place the baking dish in the air fryer basket. Slice and serve.

Moist Pumpkin Muffins

Preparation Time: 10 minutes Cooking Time: 15 minutes Serve: 20

Ingredients:

- 2 scoops vanilla protein powder
- 1/2 cup almond flour
- 1/2 cup coconut oil
- 1/2 cup pumpkin puree
- 1/2 cup almond butter
- 1 tbsp cinnamon
- 1 tsp baking powder

Directions:

In a large bowl, mix together all dry ingredients. Add wet ingredients into the dry ingredients and mix until well combined. Pour batter into the silicone muffin molds. Select Bake mode. Set time to 15 minutes and temperature 350 F then press START. The air fryer display will prompt you to ADD FOOD once the temperature is reached then place muffin molds in the air fryer basket. Serve and enjoy.

Healthy Zucchini Gratin

Preparation Time: 10 minutes Cooking Time: 30 minutes Serve: 4

Ingredients:

- 1 egg, lightly beaten

- 3 medium zucchinis, sliced

- 1/2 cup nutritional yeast

- 1 1/4 cup unsweetened almond milk

- 1 tbsp Dijon mustard

- 1 tsp sea salt

Directions: Arrange zucchini slices in the oven-safe casserole dish. In a saucepan, heat almond milk over low heat and stir in Dijon mustard, nutritional yeast, and sea salt. Add egg and whisk well. Pour sauce over zucchini slices. Cover dish with foil. Select Bake mode. Set time to 30 minutes and temperature 400 F then press START. The air fryer display will prompt you to ADD FOOD once the temperature is reached then place a casserole dish in the air fryer basket. Serve and enjoy.

Artichoke Quiche

Preparation Time: 10 minutes Cooking Time: 40 minutes Serve: 4

Ingredients:

- 3 eggs
- 1 cup artichoke hearts, chopped
- 1 cup mushrooms, sliced
- 1 small onion, chopped
- 3 garlic cloves, minced
- 1/2 cup cottage cheese, fat-free
- 10 oz spinach, frozen
- 1/2 tsp olive oil
- Pepper Salt

Directions: Heat oil in a pan over medium heat. Add onion, mushrooms, garlic, and spinach and sauté for a minute. In a bowl add cheese, artichoke hearts, eggs, pepper, and salt mix well. Add sautéed vegetable mixture to the bowl and mix well. Pour egg mixture into the greased baking dish. Cover dish with foil. Select Bake mode. Set time to 40 minutes and temperature 350 F then press START. The air fryer display will prompt you to ADD FOOD once the temperature is reached then place the baking dish in the air fryer basket. Serve and enjoy.

Tomato Feta Frittata

Preparation Time: 10 minutes Cooking Time: 7 minutes Serve: 2

Ingredients:

- 6 eggs

- 2/3 cup feta cheese, crumbled

- 1 small onion, chopped

- 1 tbsp fresh chives, chopped

- 1 tbsp olive oil

- 1 tbsp fresh basil, chopped

- 3 oz cherry tomatoes, halved

- Pepper Salt

Directions:

Heat oil in a pan over medium-high heat. Add onion and sauté until lightly browned. Remove from heat. In a bowl, whisk eggs, basil, chives, pepper, and salt. Stir in sauteed onion, cherry tomatoes, and crumbled cheese. Pour egg mixture into the greased baking dish. Select Broil mode. Set time to 7 minutes and temperature 400 F then press START. The air fryer display will prompt you to ADD FOOD once the temperature is reached then place the baking dish in the air fryer basket. Serve and enjoy.

Blueberry Cream Cheese Toasts

Prep + cook time: 15 minutes 2 servings

Ingredients

- 2 eggs, beaten
- 4 bread slices
- 1 tbsp sugar
- 1 ½ cups corn flakes
- 1/3 cup milk
- ¼ tsp ground nutmeg
- 4 tbsp whipped cream cheese
- 1 tbsp blueberry preserves

Directions

Preheat air fryer to 390 F. In a bowl, mix sugar, eggs, nutmeg, and milk. In a separate bowl, whisk the cream cheese and blueberry preserves. Spread the blueberry mixture on 2 bread slices. Cover with the remaining 2 slices to make sandwiches. Dip in the egg mixture, then thoroughly coat in cornflakes. Lay the sandwiches in the air fryer's basket and cook for 8 minutes, flipping once. Serve immediately.

Onion & Cheddar Omelet

Prep + cook time: 20 minutes 2 servings

Ingredients

- 4 eggs

- 3 tbsp cheddar cheese, grated

- 1 tsp soy sauce

- ½ onion, sliced

Directions

Preheat air fryer to 350 F. Whisk the eggs with soy sauce and mix in onion. Pour the egg mixture into a greased baking pan and place it in the fryer's basket. Bake for 12-14 minutes. Top with the grated cheddar cheese and serve right away. Best served with a tomato salad or freshly chopped scallions.

Spicy Egg & Bacon Tortilla Wraps

Prep + cook time: 15 minutes 3 servings

Ingredients

- 3 flour tortillas

- 2 eggs, scrambled

- 3 slices bacon, cut into strips

- 3 tbsp salsa

- 3 tbsp cream cheese

- 1 cup Pepper Jack cheese, grated

Directions

Preheat air fryer to 390 F. Spread the cream cheese on the tortillas. Add the eggs and bacon and top with salsa. Scatter over the grated cheese and roll up tightly. Place in the fryer's basket and AirFry for 10 minutes or until golden. Cut in half and serve warm.

Turkey & Mushroom Sandwich

Prep + cook time: 10 minutes 1 serving

Ingredients

- 1/3 cup leftover turkey, shredded

- 1/3 cup sliced mushrooms, sauteed

- ½ tbsp butter, softened

- 2 tomato slices

- ½ tsp red pepper flakes

- Salt and black pepper to taste

- 1 hamburger bun, halved

Directions

Preheat air fryer to 350 F. Brush the bottom half with butter and top with shredded turkey. Arrange mushroom slices on top of the turkey. Cover with tomato slices and sprinkle with salt, black pepper, and red flakes. Top with the other bun half and AirFry in the fryer for 5-8 minutes until crispy.

Grilled Tofu Sandwich with Cabbage

Prep + cook time: 20 minutes 1 serving

Ingredients

- 2 slices of bread
- 1 slice tofu,
- 1-inch thick
- ¼ cup red cabbage, shredded
- 2 tsp olive oil
- ¼ tsp vinegar
- Salt and black pepper to taste

Directions

Preheat air fryer to 350 F. Add the bread slices to the air fryer basket and toast for 3 minutes; set aside. Brush the tofu with some olive oil and place in the air fryer to Bake for 5 minutes on each side.

Mix the cabbage, remaining olive oil, and vinegar. Season with salt. Place the tofu on top of one bread slice, place the cabbage over, and top with the other bread slice. Serve with cream cheese-mustard dip.

Buttered Eggs in Hole

Prep + cook time: 15 minutes 2 servings

Ingredients

- 2 bread slices
- 2 eggs
- Salt and black pepper to taste
- 2 tbsp butter

Directions

Preheat air fryer to 360 F. Place a heatproof bowl in the fryer's basket and brush with butter. Make a hole in the middle of the bread slices with a bread knife and place on the heatproof bowl in 2 batches. Crack an egg into the center of each hole; season. Bake in the air fryer for 4 minutes. Turn the bread with a spatula and cook for another 4 minutes. Serve warm.

Loaded Egg Pepper Rings

Prep + cook time: 15 minutes 4 servings

Ingredients

- 4 eggs
- 1 bell pepper, cut into four
- ¾-inch rings
- 5 cherry tomatoes, halved
- Salt and black pepper to taste

Directions

Preheat air fryer to 360 F. Put the bell pepper rings in a greased baking pan and crack an egg into each one. Season with salt and pepper. Top with the halved cherry tomatoes. Put the pan into the air fryer and air fry for 6-9 minutes, or until the eggs are have set. Serve and enjoy!

Chili Hash Browns

Prep + cook time: 25 minutes + cooling time 4 servings

Ingredients

- 1 lb potatoes, peeled and shredded
- Salt and black pepper to taste
- 1 tsp garlic powder
- 1 tsp chili flakes
- 1 tsp onion powder
- 1 egg, beaten
- 1 tbsp olive oil
- Cooking spray

Directions

Heat olive oil in a skillet over medium heat and sauté potatoes for 10 minutes; transfer to a bowl. After they have cooled, add in the egg, pepper, salt, chili flakes, onion powder, and garlic powder and mix well. On a flat plate, spread the mixture and pat it firmly with your fingers. Refrigerate for 20 minutes. Preheat air fryer to 350 F. Shape the cooled into patties. Grease the air fryer basket with cooking spray and arrange the patties in. Cook for 12 minutes on AirFry mode, flipping once. Serve warm.

Japanese-Style Omelet

Prep + cook time: 20 minutes 1 serving

Ingredients

- 1 cup cubed tofu

- 3 whole eggs

- Salt and black pepper to taste

- ¼ tsp ground coriander

- ¼ tsp cumin

- 1 tsp soy sauce

- 1 tbsp green onions, chopped

- ¼ onion, chopped

Directions

In a bowl, mix eggs, onion, soy sauce, coriander, cumin, black pepper, and salt. Add in cubed tofu and pour the mixture into a greased baking tray. Place in the air fryer and Bake for 8 minutes at 400 F. When ready, remove, and sprinkle with green onions to serve.

Baked Kale Omelet

Prep + cook time: 15 minutes 2 servings

Ingredients

- 5 eggs

- 3 tbsp cottage cheese, crumbled

- 1 cup kale, chopped

- ½ tbsp fresh basil, chopped

- ½ tbsp fresh parsley, chopped

- Salt and black pepper to taste

Directions

Beat the eggs, salt, and pepper in a bowl. Stir in the rest of the ingredients. Pour the mixture into a greased baking pan and fit in the air fryer. Bake for 10 minutes at 330 F until slightly golden and set.

Baked Avocado with Eggs & Cilantro

Prep + cook time: 10 minutes 1 serving

Ingredients

- 1 ripe avocado, pitted and halved
- 2 eggs Salt and black pepper, to taste
- 1 tsp fresh cilantro, chopped

Directions

Preheat air fryer to 400 F. Crack one egg into each avocado half and place in the air fryer. Bake for 8-12 minutes until the eggs are cooked through. Sprinkle with salt and black pepper and let cool slightly. Top with freshly chopped cilantro and serve warm.

Cheese Egg Quiche

Preparation Time: 10 minutes Cooking Time: 45 minutes Serve: 6

Ingredients:

- 8 eggs

- 6 oz cheddar cheese, shredded

- 5 tbsp butter, melted

- 6 oz cream cheese

Directions:

Add eggs, cheese, butter, and cream cheese into the mixing bowl and blend using a hand mixer until well combined. Pour egg mixture into the greased pie dish. Cover dish with foil. Select Bake mode. Set time to 45 minutes and temperature 325 F then press START. The air fryer display will prompt you to ADD FOOD once the temperature is reached then place the pie dish in the air fryer basket. Serve and enjoy.

Chorizo Casserole

Preparation Time: 10 minutes Cooking Time: 55 minutes Serve: 6

Ingredients:

- 8 eggs

- 1 cup cheddar cheese, shredded

- 1 bell pepper, diced

- 4 oz can green chiles, drained and chopped

- 3/4 cup heavy cream

- 1/2 lb ground chorizo sausage

- 1/4 tsp pepper

- 1/2 tsp salt

Directions:

Cook chorizo in a pan over medium-high heat for 8 minutes or until browned. In a bowl, whisk eggs with cream, pepper, and salt. Stir in cooked chorizo, cheese, bell pepper, and green chiles. Pour egg mixture into the greased baking dish. Cover dish with foil. Select Bake mode. Set time to 40 minutes and temperature 350 F then press START. The air fryer display will prompt you to ADD FOOD once the temperature is reached then place the baking dish in the air fryer basket. Serve and enjoy.

Sausage Egg Omelet

Preparation Time: 10 minutes Cooking Time: 30 minutes Serve: 12

Ingredients:

- 7 eggs

- 1 lb breakfast sausage

- 1 tsp mustard

- 3/4 cup heavy whipping cream

- 1/4 onion, chopped

- 2 cups cheddar cheese, shredded

- 1/2 bell pepper, chopped

- 1/4 tsp pepper

- 1/2 tsp salt

Directions:

Add sausage into the pan and cook until brown, add onion and bell pepper and cook for 2 minutes. In a bowl, whisk eggs with 1 1/2 cups cheddar cheese, cream, mustard, pepper, and salt. Stir in sausage mixture. Pour egg mixture into the greased 9*13-inch baking dish. Top with remaining cheese. Cover dish with foil. Select Bake mode. Set time to 20 minutes and temperature 350 F then press START. The air fryer display will prompt you to ADD FOOD once the temperature is reached then place the baking dish in the air fryer basket. Serve and enjoy.

Cheese Ham Egg Muffins

Preparation Time: 10 minutes Cooking Time: 20 minutes Serve: 12

Ingredients:

- 12 eggs
- 1 3/4 cup cheddar cheese, shredded
- 2 cups ham, diced
- 1 tsp garlic, minced
- 1/2 pepper
- 1/2 tsp salt

Directions:

In a bowl, whisk eggs with garlic, pepper, and salt. Stir in cheddar cheese and ham. Pour egg mixture into the silicone muffin molds. Select Bake mode. Set time to 20 minutes and temperature 375 F then press START. The air fryer display will prompt you to ADD FOOD once the temperature is reached then place muffin molds in the air fryer basket. Serve and enjoy.

Perfect Baked Omelet

Preparation Time: 10 minutes Cooking Time: 45 minutes Serve: 6

Ingredients:

- 8 eggs

- 1 cup bell pepper, chopped

- 1/2 cup onion, chopped

- 1/2 cup cheddar cheese, shredded

- 6 oz cooked ham, diced

- 1 cup unsweetened almond milk

- 1/2 tsp salt

Directions:

In a bowl, whisk eggs with milk and salt. Stir in bell pepper, onion, cheese, and ham. Pour egg mixture into the greased 8-inch baking dish. Select Bake mode. Set time to 45 minutes and temperature 350 F then press START. The air fryer display will prompt you to ADD FOOD once the temperature is reached then place the baking dish in the air fryer basket. Serve and enjoy.

Broccoli Casserole

Preparation Time: 10 minutes Cooking Time: 20 minutes Serve: 4

Ingredients:

- 2 cups broccoli florets, chopped
- 1 cup cheddar cheese, grated
- 1/2 cup sour cream
- 1/2 cup heavy cream
- Pepper Salt

Directions:

In a bowl, whisk together heavy cream, sour cream, 1/2 cheddar cheese, pepper, and salt. Add broccoli florets into the baking dish. Pour heavy cream mixture over broccoli. Top with remaining cheese. Cover baking dish with foil. Select Bake mode. Set time to 20 minutes and temperature 350 F then press START. The air fryer display will prompt you to ADD FOOD once the temperature is reached then place the baking dish in the air fryer basket. Serve and enjoy

THANK YOU

Thank you for choosing *Quick & Easy Recipes for Breakfast* for improving your cooking skills! I hope you enjoyed making the recipes as much as tasting them! If you're interested in learning new recipes and new meals to cook, go and check out the other books of the series.

Lightning Source UK Ltd.
Milton Keynes UK
UKHW020211080521
383350UK00003B/372